HORSE POWER

SPARKY'S STEM GUIDE TO

CARS

BY KIRSTY HOLMES

KidHaven
PUBLISHING

Published in 2023 by **KidHaven Publishing,
an Imprint of Greenhaven Publishing, LLC**
29 East 21st Street
New York, NY 10010

Edited by: Emilie Dufresne
Designed by: Danielle Rippengill

Cataloging-in-Publication Data

Names: Holmes, Kirsty.
Title: Sparky's STEM guide to cars / Kirsty Holmes.
Description: New York : KidHaven Publishing, 2023. | Series:
Horse power | Includes glossary and index.
Identifiers: ISBN 9781534540255 (pbk.) | ISBN 9781534540279
(library bound) | ISBN 9781534540262
(6 pack) | ISBN 9781534540286 (ebook)
Subjects: LCSH: Automobiles--Juvenile literature.
Classification: LCC TL23.H635 2023 | DDC 629.222--dc23

Printed in the United States of America

CPSIA compliance information: Batch #CSKH23: For further information contact Greenhaven Publishing
LLC, New York, New York at 1-844-317-7404.

Please visit our website, www.greenhavenpublishing.com. For a free
color catalog of all our high-quality books, call toll free 1-844-317-7404
or fax 1-844-317-7405.

IMAGE CREDITS

*All images are courtesy of Shutterstock.com, unless otherwise specified. With thanks to Getty Images, Thinkstock Photo and iStockphoto.
Cover – NotionPic, A–R–T, logika600, BiterBig, miniaria, Macrovector. Sparky – NotionPic, Macrovector. Peggy – NotionPic. Grid – BiterBig.
Driving School – Mascha Tace. 2 – Viktor96. 5 – Mascha Tace. 6 – miniaria, EgudinKa, Ivan Paal. 7 – studioworkstock, Viktor96. 8 & 9 – Viktor96.
10 – Pretty Vectors. 11 – Viktor96. 12 – VectorMine. 13 – miniaria, Mascha Tace. 14 – Fleren. 15 – VoodooDot, RedKoala. 16 & 17 – Wth. 18 – Mascha Tace,
VectorShow, miniaria. 19 – Igogosha. 20 – Mascha Tace. 22 – Alexandr III, Icon Craft Studio. 23 – Viktor96, GraphicsRF.*

CONTENTS

WORDS THAT LOOK LIKE <u>this</u> CAN BE FOUND IN THE GLOSSARY ON PAGE 24.

WELCOME TO DRIVING SCHOOL!

HELLO! I'm Jeremy Sparkplug, world-famous racing driver. You can call me Sparky. You must be the new recruits. Welcome to the Horses for Courses School of Motoring!

HORSES FOR COURSES
SCHOOL
U
EARN YOUR HORSESHOES

HORSE POWER

HORSE POWER
U
1

Here you will be learning about some of the coolest **vehicles** on four wheels. If you pass your driving test, you'll earn your Golden Horseshoe. So pay attention: it's time to DRIVE!

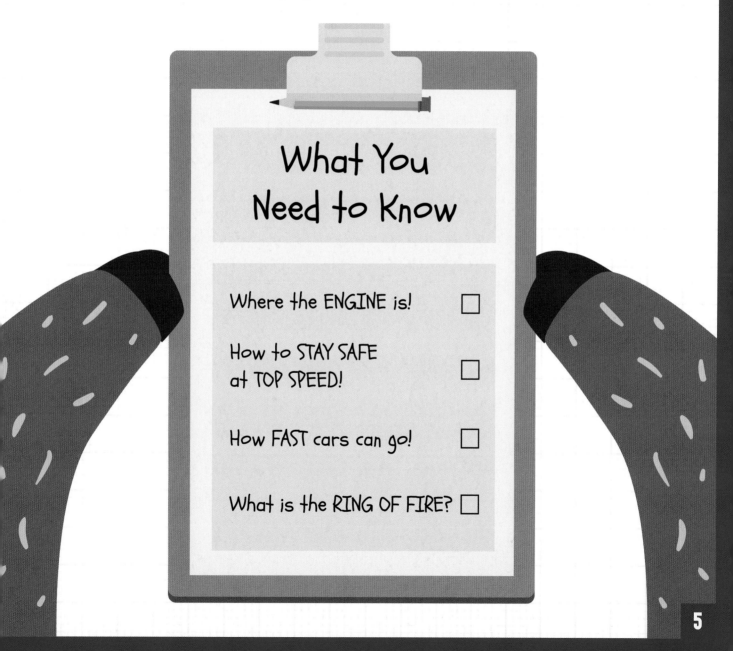

What You Need to Know

Where the ENGINE is! ☐

How to STAY SAFE at TOP SPEED! ☐

How FAST cars can go! ☐

What is the RING OF FIRE? ☐

Lesson 1: WHAT IS A CAR?

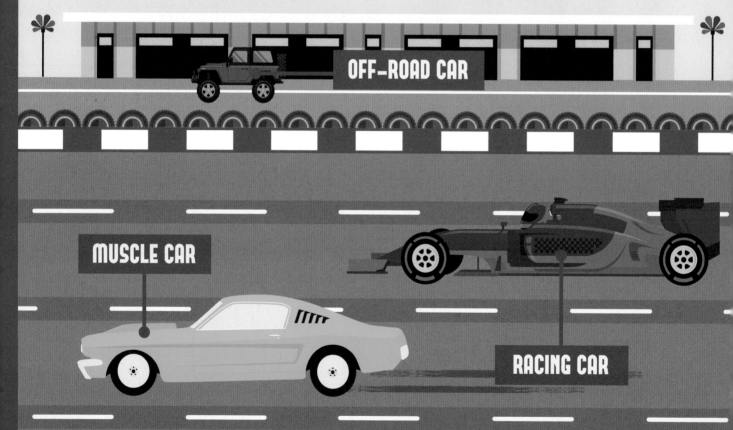

OFF-ROAD CAR

MUSCLE CAR

RACING CAR

A car is a type of <u>passenger</u> vehicle. Cars drive mostly on roads, can seat up to eight people, and usually have four wheels.

SPORTS CAR

FAMILY CAR

Class, meet Peggy. Some people don't believe she exists. All I know is, she can really drive!

PARTS OF A CAR

SIDE-VIEW MIRRORS

Drivers use these to see behind them.

Let's look at the parts of a car.

TIRES

Tires are made of **rubber**. A special pattern, called a tread, helps the tires grip the road.

ENGINE

The engine uses **fuel** to create energy to power the car.

LIGHTS

These are for driving at night and to show when you are turning or stopping.

WINDSHIELD

This is a glass window at the front of the car.

EXHAUST

Any waste **gases** come out here.

SPARKY 1

BUMPERS

These stop low-speed accidents from causing too much damage.

SPARKY 1

LICENSE PLATE

This shows a special code that is different for each car.

LESSON 3:
INSIDE A CAR

FUEL GAUGE
Measures fuel

SPEEDOMETER
Measures speed

GPS
Tells you where to go

STEERING WHEEL
Turns the car

IGNITION
Starts the car

HANDBRAKE
Holds the car still when parked

PEDALS
Help to change gear, speed up, and brake

GEARSTICK
Changes gear

Inside a car, there are controls on the dashboard and on the floor by the driver. There are also instruments that give the driver important information.

The driver sits on the right-hand side in some countries, and on the left-hand side in others. The driver's seat is usually opposite the side of the road they drive on, so the driver is nearer the middle of the road.

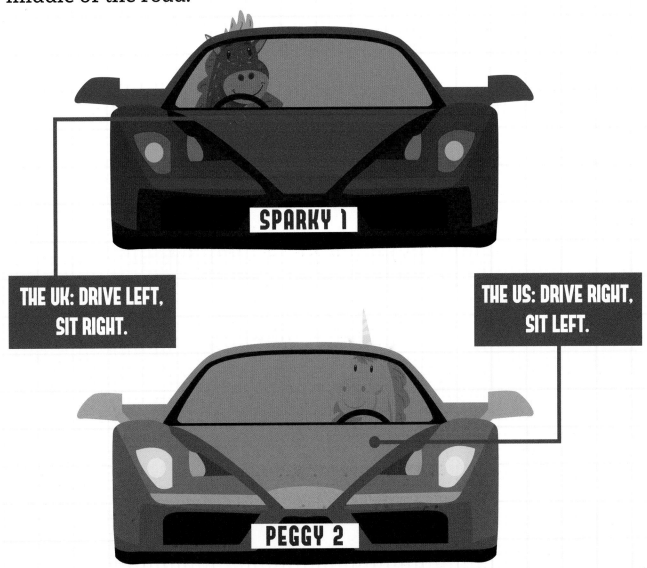

THE UK: DRIVE LEFT, SIT RIGHT.

THE US: DRIVE RIGHT, SIT LEFT.

SPARKY 1

PEGGY 2

ENGINES!

Combustion engines use small explosions from fuel to make **pistons** move up and down. This makes the wheels turn.

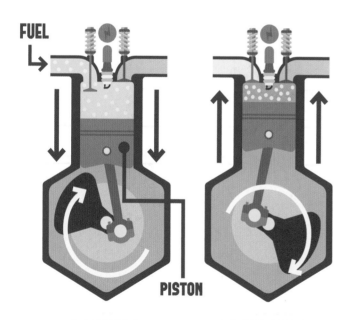
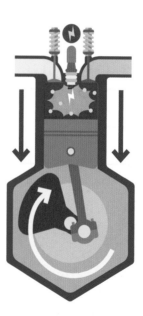
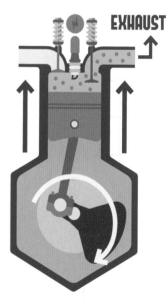

FUEL

EXHAUST

PISTON

1. SUCK
Air and fuel go in.

2. SQUEEZE
The mixture is squashed.

3. BANG
A small explosion pushes the piston.

4. BLOW
Waste gases are pushed out.

An electric car is powered by an electric motor and a battery. These need to be charged up at a special socket, a bit like a smartphone.

FORMULA E – ALL-ELECTRIC RACING

COFFEE & PIES

ICE COLD DRINKS

OPEN

POWERED BY ELECTRICITY!

LESSON 5:
SAFETY!

Did you know that the first cars didn't have seat belts?
Don't worry – although nobody wants to be in a car accident,
modern cars have lots of clever ways to keep us safe.

14

SAFETY FEATURES

AIRBAG

A bag inflates and keeps you from banging your head inside the car.

SEAT BELT

A strap holds you in your seat in case there is a crash.

BABY CARRIERS

Babies should face backward in a special car seat.

CHILD SEATS

Older children should use a booster seat until they are around 12.

HEAD RESTRAINTS

These keep your head from snapping back and protect your neck.

CRUMPLE ZONE

The front of the car squashes easily, so the passenger is protected.

LESSON 6:
THE NEED FOR SPEED!

Some of the fastest cars around are the sleek, speedy race cars of **Formula 1** (F1) racing. They are built to be light, low to the ground, and very aerodynamic. Let's look at what that means.

Because the car is so low, air can pass over the top and push the car toward the ground. The wedge-like shape helps the car cut through the air.

THE AIR PUSHES DOWNWARD ON THE CAR, HELPING IT STICK TO THE ROAD AND NOT TIP OVER.

LESSON 7: COOL CARS

THRUST SSC

The Thrust Supersonic Car has held the land speed record since 1997. It made a top speed of 763.034 miles (1,227.985 km) per hour and was the first land vehicle to go faster than the speed of sound.

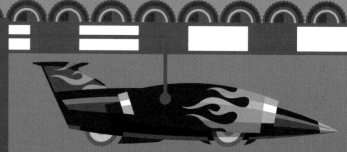

BAR-HONDA 067 LAKESTER

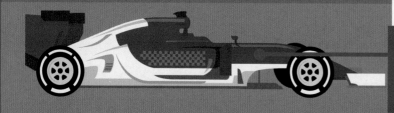

The fastest F1 car ever, the 067 Lakester, reached 256.6 miles (413 km) per hour.

LONGEST CAR EVER

At 100 feet (30.5 m) long, with 26 wheels, Jay Ohrberg's limousine holds the world record for longest car. It has its own small swimming pool.

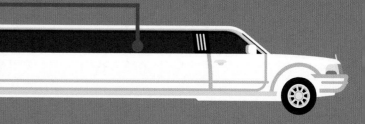

THE SMALLEST CAR

PEEL P50

The smallest road car ever made, the P50, was made for "one adult and a shopping bag." Only 50 were ever made.

SPARKY 2

DRIVING TEST

Buckle up, learners. Time to gallop through your driving test and see if you're an ace racer – or whether you've just been horsing around! (Check your answers on page 21!)

Questions

1. What are car tires usually made of?

2. What does the ignition do?

3. What are the four stages in a combustion engine?

4. What should all passengers in a car always wear?

5. How fast was the Thrust SSC?

Did you get all the answers right?

Of course you did – here is your Golden Horseshoe.
You are now an ace racing driver, just like Peggy and me!

THE RING OF FIRE!

Stunt drivers perform terrifying tricks and death-defying feats of daring in their cars. It takes years of training, but we're professionals, so let us show you how it's done...

STEP ONE
Get stunt car

STEP TWO
Safety checks

STEP THREE
Matches

STEP FOUR

GO GO GO!

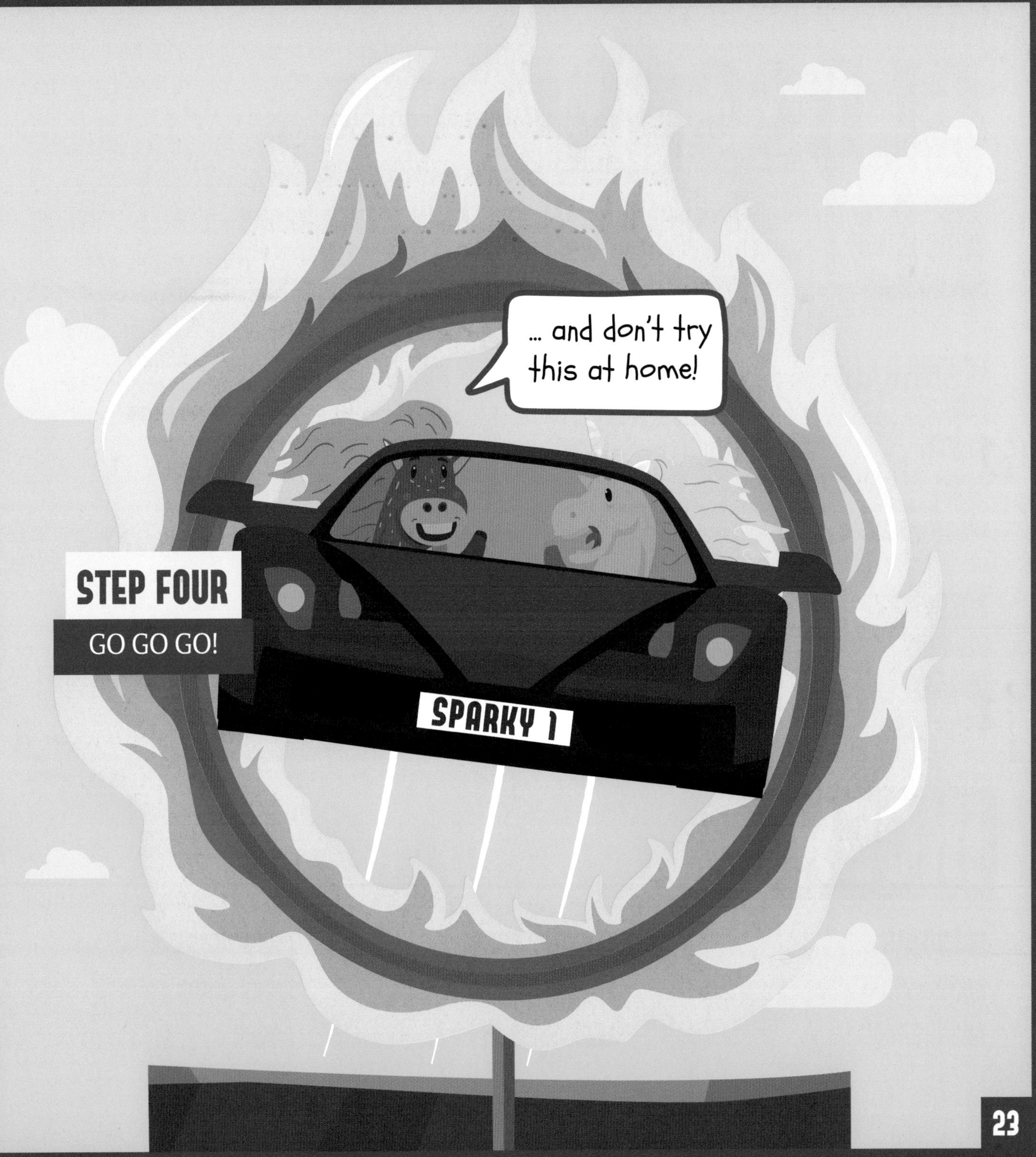

GLOSSARY

COMBUSTION — the act of burning or setting fire to something

DASHBOARD — the panel facing the driver of a vehicle that contains the controls for driving

FORMULA 1 — a popular motor vehicle racing competition

FUEL — a material used to make heat or power

GASES — things that are like air and fill any space available

GEAR — part of a machine that makes other parts move

INSTRUMENTS — devices that measure something, such as speed or the amount of fuel

PASSENGER — someone who rides in a vehicle but is not the driver

PISTONS — pieces of machinery that move up and down in a car engine

RUBBER — a bouncy material made from tropical plants

VEHICLES — machines used for carrying or transporting things or people

INDEX